# HISTORY *on your* DOORSTEP

written by
Jane Launchbury and Selma Montford

illustrated by Jane Launchbury

YOUNG LIBRARY

# Be Streetwise

**Towns are exciting places to explore, but they can be dangerous. All detectives need to be properly briefed and equipped.**

Always tell an adult where you are going, how you are getting there, and when you expect to be back.

Wear a watch so you don't need to ask what the time is. Check opening times. Always let a parent know if you are delayed.

Take enough money for your return fare, and both change and a Phonecard for phone calls.

Don't talk to strangers. Before you go out, talk to an adult about who to ask for help in an emergency. (These may include police officers, traffic wardens, bus drivers, and post office, bank or station staff).

Keep your hand or foot against your belongings.

If you have a bicycle, learn how to use it safely.

Never play on building sites, on roads or on other people's property.

Try not to go out alone, and be home before dark.

Learn how to use a public phone, and how to make reverse charge and 999 calls.

Have an up-to-date map, and check transport timetables.

Never accept lifts or invitations into private buildings, even if you are very tired or lost.

Know the Green Cross Code. Read the Highway Code.

Always look where you are going. Don't walk along looking up at buildings, or step backwards into the road.

Never drop litter. Look for a bin or take it home with you.

**Above all, use your common sense.**

First Published in hard cover 1990
This edition published in paperback 1995
YOUNG LIBRARY LTD
3 The Old Brushworks
56 Pickwick Road
Corsham Wiltshire SN13 9BX



ISBN 1-85429-050-9

Printed in China

# Contents

# Home Base History

How old are you? Quite a lot of history has happened since you were born. Things don't have to be old to have a history. Yesterday was history. How old is your home? Even if it is a modern one, there is still history on your doorstep.

Walk around your home and look carefully for clues to the past. Are there any bricked-up fireplaces? Can you see old 5-amp power sockets or sealed gas pipes? Is there more than one layer of wallpaper or other colours of paint where a top layer has been chipped? A chimney stack with chimney pots, or have they been removed? Little things like this are clues to the way your home used to be, just what an urban detective needs.

Perhaps someone in your family took photographs of the home years ago. These can be interesting. Try to take some photographs of your own, or make drawings of your home, inside and out. In a few years these will be historic documents. Things change fast these days.

Who owned your home before you did? For most houses, papers called 'deeds' can tell you this. They contain details about the land the house stands on, the dates it was sold, and the names of the buyers. The records go back a number of years. Ask a parent whether they have a copy of the 'deeds'.

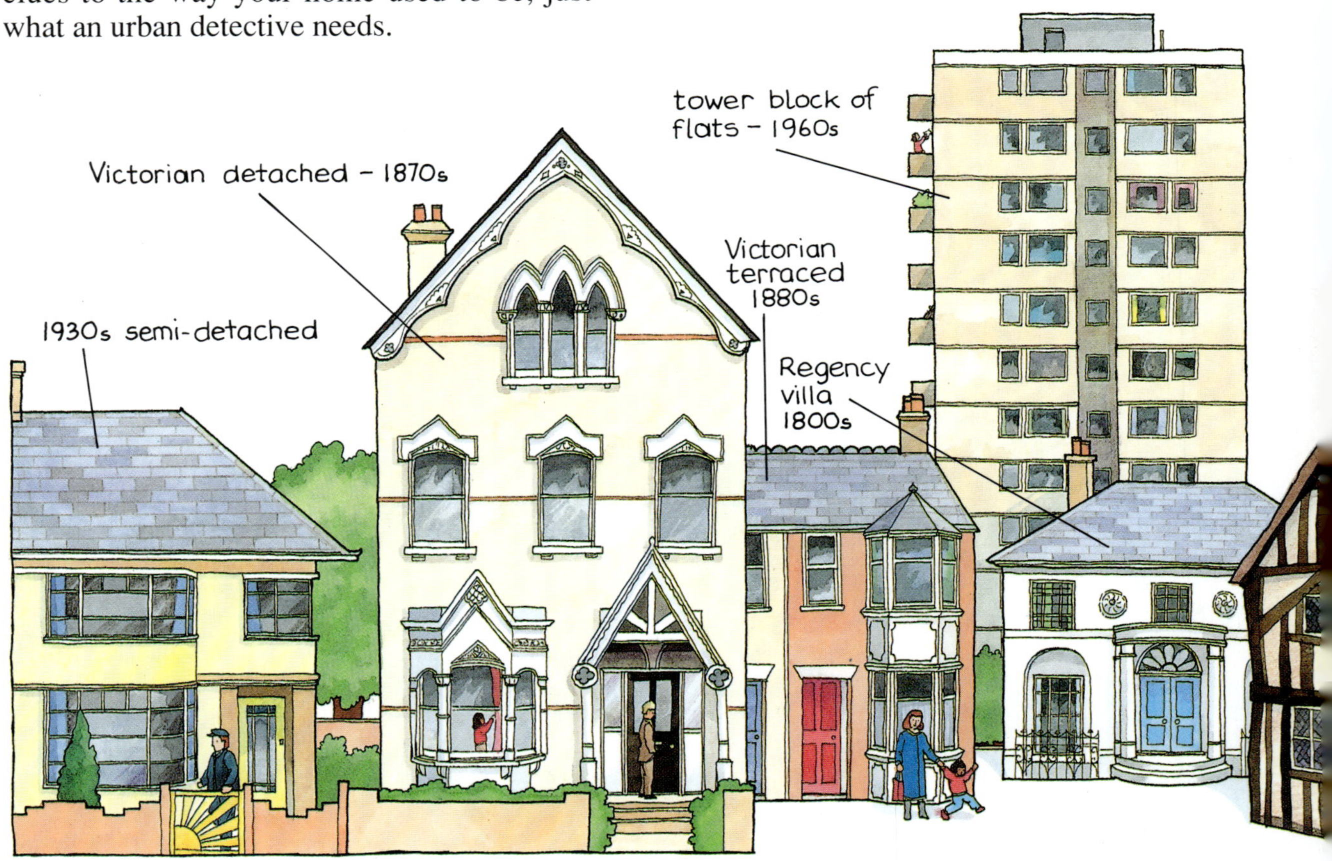

Revolution, the First World War, and the first gramophone records and automatic telephones.

People of ninety would remember the coronations of Edward VIII and George V, the suffragettes, the first motor buses, and the race between Scott and Amundsen to reach the South Pole.

Where should the interview take place? People are usually most relaxed and talkative in their own homes, so ask if you may come and visit them. A lot of old people are lonely and do not need much persuasion.

Try to find out a little about the person beforehand. If you can take along any old photos of the period they could be a useful key to unlocking someone's memory.

When interviewing an old person, speak slowly and clearly, and always be polite. Very old people often tell you the same story more than once. Try to look interested - then ask a different question to bring them back to the subject. Do not press for information which may be upsetting, like the deaths of children. As old people sometimes tire easily choose the right moment to end the interview. If you still have some more questions, ask if you may visit again in a few days' time.

Very old people's memories work strangely. Often they cannot remember what they did yesterday, but ask them about their childhood and you can't fail!

Sometimes it can help to interview two or three people together. They might encourage each other to swap stories. You may be able to visit an old people's home or day centre, which could be very rewarding.

After the interview, do not forget to write and thank the old people for giving up their time and sharing their memories.

## Grilling the Witnesses

Before you interview adults, practise on some of your friends. Of course, they won't be able to tell you about times long ago, but events of yesterday will do for practise. Choose a subject like play, homes, food, or favourite TV programmes. Don't ask questions with 'yes' or 'no' answers; you won't find out much that way. Don't talk too much or argue, and try not to express your own opinion. Look interested - encourage the speaker with nods and smiles, and react to what you are being told. If the interview works well with a friend it will probably work well when you do it 'for real'.

It can be good fun to use a cassette recorder if you have one. Afterwards write up notes from the tape on to paper. If you don't have a recorder take notes by hand during the interview. Don't forget to make a record of the date, place and names, addresses and 'phone numbers of the people involved. Write this on your paper or cassette box.

# Local Intelligence

To solve the mysteries of history, detectives need good sources of information. Luckily for you, your sources are all near by, and most people will be pleased to help.

What do you want to investigate? Is it your home itself, the street, neighbourhood or whole town?

Perhaps it is the architecture, archaeology, or people that interest you most. What kind of time span do you want to investigate? Victorian times? When your mum and dad were children? Last year? Don't forget that history is being made today. There may be big changes taking place in your town now. A record of what is happening now could be a useful historical document in a few years' time.

How much time can you afford? Don't be too ambitious. It is better to do a small investigation thoroughly than a large one on which you only scratch the surface.

Have you any pocket money to spend on being an urban detective? You will have expenses: fares, 'phone calls, notebooks, card index ... It will add up.

Start by looking at what you have already at home. Does your family get the local newspaper, for example? You could start a cuttings collection on a topic such as the football team, or conservation of fine old buildings. The paper may also run a local history section or photos of the old days. Perhaps your family has old photographs or maps of the area?

For tips about storing all these things, see Book 1 page 22. Detectives must keep their information organized!

Local libraries are generally full of historical evidence. Most have a local history section. The librarians will help you, but don't forget your 'please' and 'thank you' and behave quietly.

Things to look for include the journals of local history societies, a guide to your local record office, street directories, museum guides, old newspapers, tourist leaflets, and maps (see page 10 for more about maps). Perhaps they also have a collection of historic photos, prints, and postcards. You could make photocopies of them. Finally they can tell you about other local information sources.

Do you have a local museum? This can be an excellent source of information. Or there may be a heritage centre or even an urban studies centre. People who work in these places are keen to help you.

There are clues to the past all around you. Learn to recognize them. For example, road or house names (see page19 - It's all in a name?) can often tell you something. Different styles of architecture can be clues to the past. A good detective learns to uncover evidence, and deduce facts, from the tiniest clues.

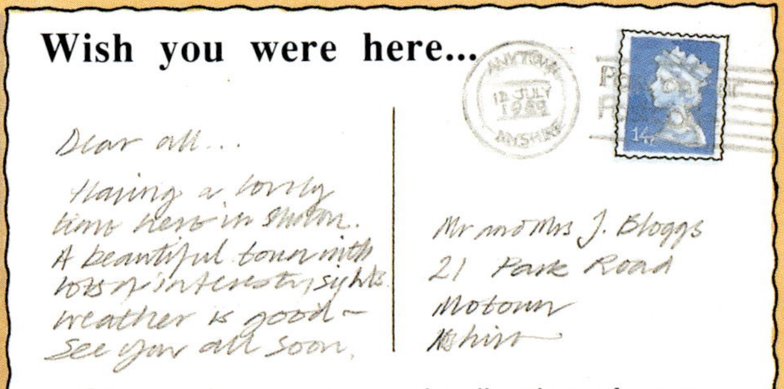


Start a picture postcard collection of your town. Find old cards in jumble sales and junk shops. Buy new ones too - they'll soon become history!

# All Kinds of Map

Looking at a map is a bit like peering through a telescope. It shows things you would not normally see. Telescopes will show you what is far away. So will maps, but they will also show you clues to the past.

Look at maps you have at home. There might be an atlas with maps of countries throughout the world; a book of road maps for when you go out in the car; a street map of your own town.

Now visit your local library. It should have several kinds of map. They come in various scales. 'Scale' means the difference in size between the map and the area it represents. For a very large area the scale must be **small** - perhaps 1 cm representing 200 km. For a small area the scale can be very **large** - perhaps 1 cm representing only 1 km.

An airport runway 2 kilometres long might be shown on the map as 1 centimetre long. There are three ways of showing this scale as in the box below:

**A**

1 cm = 2 km

*This is the simplest to understand*

**B**

1 : 20,000.

*This means that 1 = 20,000 (i.e. 20,000 centimetres, which is 2 kilometres).*

**C**

0 2 4 6 8 10 12 km

*The distance between each of the marks is a centimetre. Each mark represents 2 kilometres.*

There is a government department which makes maps of Britain. It is called Ordnance Survey. Ordnance Survey maps are drawn in great detail. They don't only show modern roads and buildings. They show relics of the past which can still be seen on the ground today. If you are clever, you can use these clues to work out what a place looked like in the past. Look for clues like hill forts, Roman roads, castles, disused railways, old mines, and so on.

Look for other kinds of map in the library.

You might find:

**tourist maps** for favourite spots in the Lake District,

**geological maps** to show what the ground under our feet is made of,

**historical maps** to show what Britain looked like during Roman times, or the Iron Age.

See how many other kinds of map you can find. They can all provide the urban detective with clues to history.

## Make your own Map

Go for a short walk with a pencil and paper. Make a map of the streets around your home. You will find it much more difficult than you think!

Include all interesting features such as shops, telephone boxes, traffic lights, bridges, and one-way streets.

Don't forget to show the scale and direction in one corner.

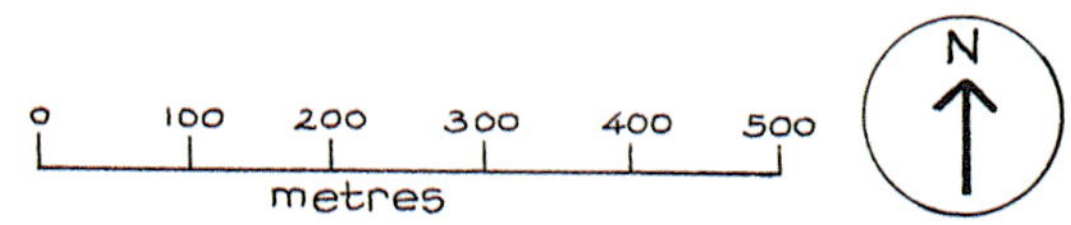

# Mapping the Changes



People have been making maps for centuries. As towns in real life change and develop, so each new map will be different. Only 400 years ago maps of Britain did not show roads at all! They showed towns and wealthy estates and the homes of important people. But few people made long journeys in those days, and they were expected to know the roads and paths in their own town. So map makers did not bother to draw in the roads.

Everything changes very quickly these days. New motorways are constructed, towns will grow larger, and bridges will be built. Maps always have a date on them. Collect Ordnance Survey maps of various dates covering the same area. Compare them. What do you see?

What about *really* old maps - 200 years old or more? The librarian probably won't let you handle them, but there will be photocopies. You will probably be allowed to photocopy these for yourself too. Look for clues to the way your town grew and developed. Are the buildings mostly at crossroads? Can you recognize things like fords, mills, and the gates of town walls?

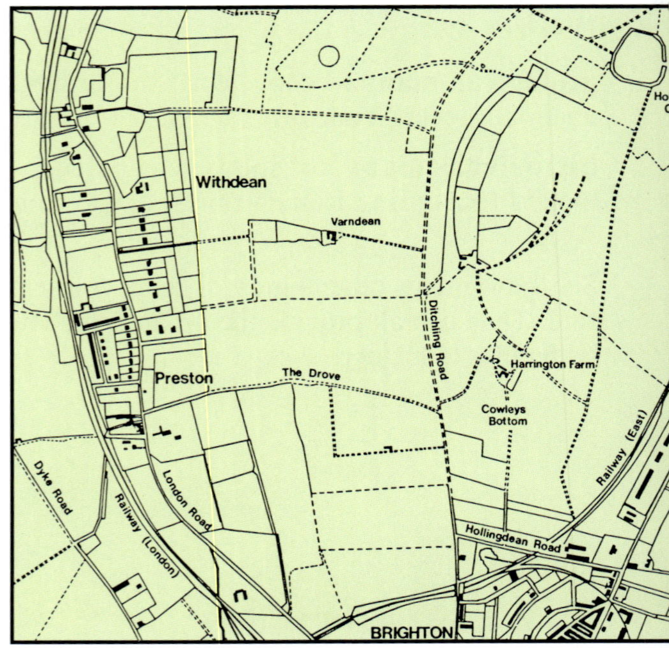

**Spot the Differences**

Try to find a series of maps of the same scale and area, but with different dates.

Trace a part of each of these on to separate sheets of tracing paper. Lay them on top of each other and try to match them up. What clues to past changes can you see?

Notice the way that pathways become roadways, and how each map shows the number of buildings increasing.

The old field boundaries can still be seen in the new road pattern. Some of the open spaces have remained the same.

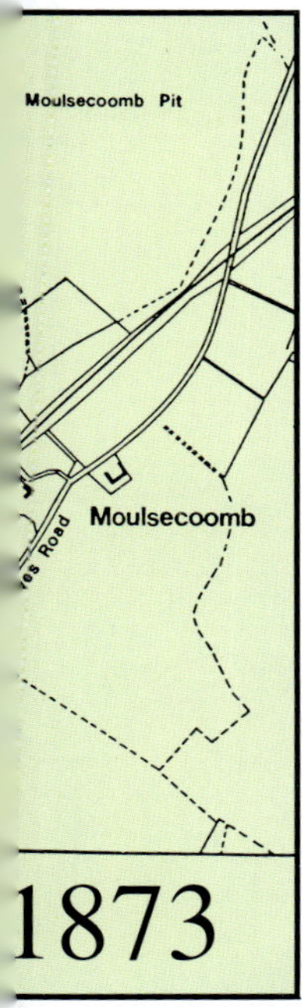


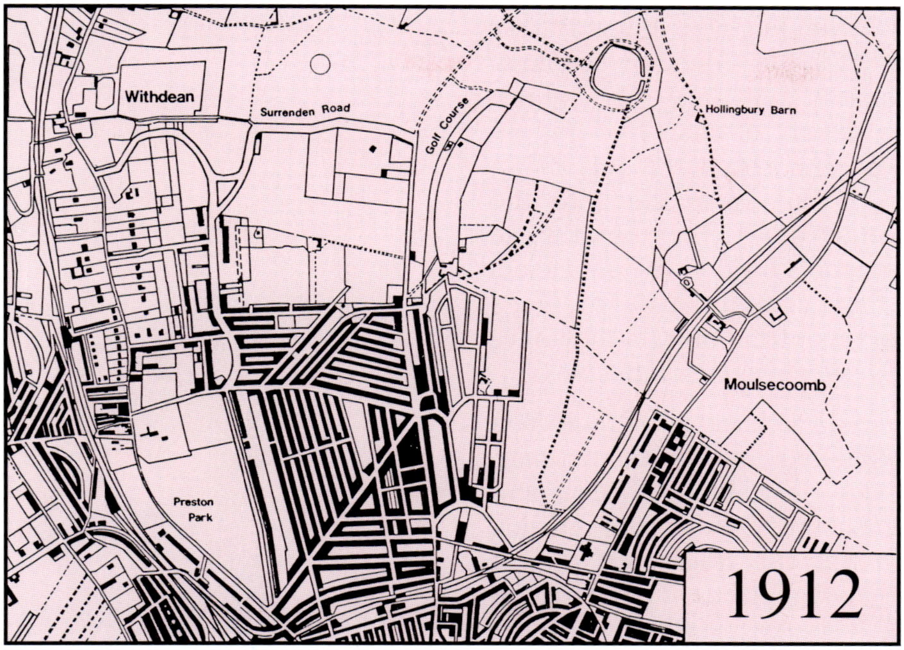


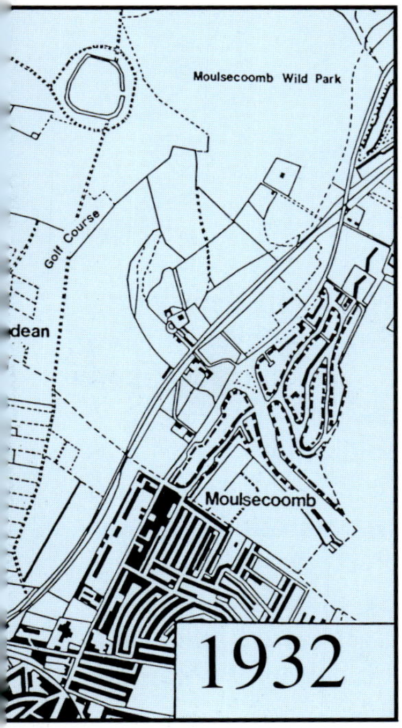


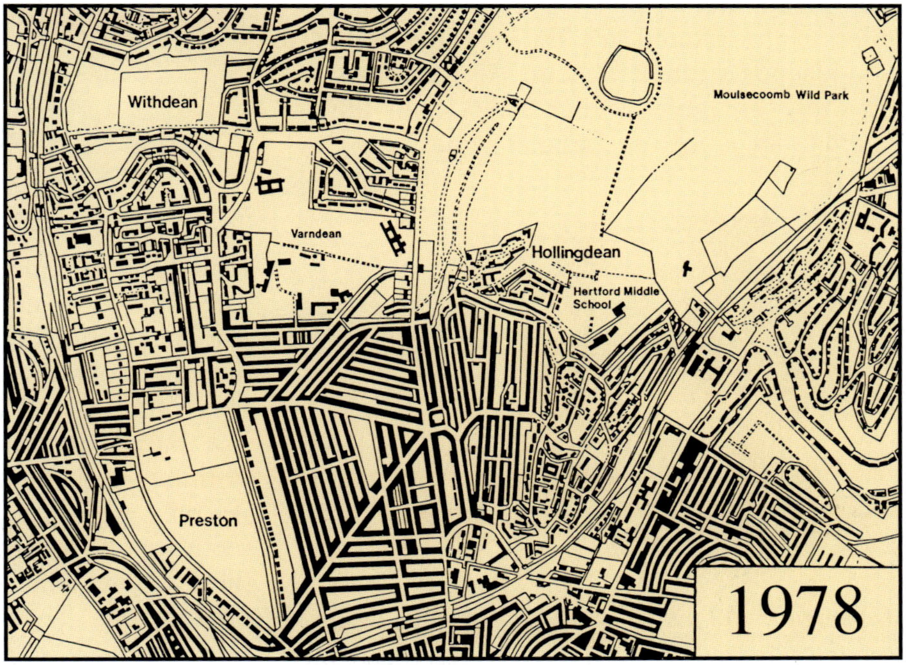

# Digging up the Past

Let's look for buried treasure! Gold and silver and jewels? Well, you might be lucky! But we mean anything left in the ground by people of the past. These 'treasures' are clues. Detectives who search for clues like this are called archaeologists. It is the job of an archaeologist to find these clues to the mysteries of former times. They build up an idea about how people used to live in ancient times. Often they actually have to piece together broken bits of the objects they have found, just like a detective does with clues.

What sort of clues do archaeologists find? You can see by walking into your nearest museum. Pottery, tools, jewelery, bones, seeds, and coins are a few examples. Others are remains of roads and walls, tile fragments, drains, rubbish heaps, and fireplaces. They look for the tiniest clues, very, very carefully. Even a single seed can tell them a lot when it is examined under a microscope. The shapes of holes in the ground left by long-ago rotted wooden posts interest them. Archaeologists are more excited by such finds than they would be by a box of smuggler's gold!

*Broken pieces of pottery are matched like a jigsaw and glued together. Plaster fills missing areas.*

How do archaeologists go about their work? They first learn a lot by studying history. They use imagination and guesswork too, just like a detective solving a crime! Then they dig very, very carefully into the soil, a few centimetres at a time. If they're lucky they uncover layers of things buried long ago under dust and soil. As they work these detectives observe and record everything. They make notes, draw pictures and plans, take measurements and photographs. Then they clean and store their finds carefully.

It is important not to destroy the evidence. Sadly, clues are often destroyed by building works. An excavator digging foundations for an office block can uncover an unknown ancient site. Sometimes all work stops for a few weeks so that archaeologists can excavate the site. If this happens in a town centre, you can sometimes peep in through a special hole in the fence to watch a 'rescue dig'.

Look closely at local building sites. You should not go on to them, but you may be able to see workmen digging trenches. Sometimes you can see remains of earlier buildings or roads. If you see anything really exciting, you should tell the local museum.

You should never dig or use a metal detector on sites of historic interest. But look around your own garden if you have one. Even things that were buried quite recently can be interesting finds. Glass bottles, clay pipes, and broken pottery and toys are quite common finds. In the days before dustmen called, people buried all sorts of things in their yards and gardens. Keep careful records of anything you find, just like the real archaeologists.

## Time Capsule

Provide evidence of present times for future archaeologists. Choose everyday objects like newspaper cuttings, coins, a video tape, an old clockwork watch, an empty drink can, a plastic carrier bag, a computer disc, and put them in a water and airtight container. Write a note with your name and date, then seal and bury your 'time capsule'.

# Tripping over the Evidence

Next time you trip on the pavement, stop and look down. You might have stumbled on something interesting! First, look for hole covers set into the pavement. Some tell you what they are for. Others have pretty patterns. Some even have dates on. Look for circular coal-hole covers. How do you think they were used and why?

Next, look beside old gateways and front doors. There are often clues here. Can you find an old footscraper? Why do you think they were needed in the past? You might also see a mounting block. What do you think it was used for? Some houses had patterned tiles outside and on their steps. Look for one of these and try to draw the pattern. If you find identical tiles at other houses, what does it tell you about the age of the houses?

In Victorian times shops often had their names written in patterned tiles on the pavement. Can you find an example? Sometimes these tiles are the only clue to the original name of the shop and what it sold. The shop may have closed years ago.

Can you find any evidence of the days when transport was horse-drawn? If you found a mounting block, you are doing well. Look at the roadside and pavement by old arches and gateways. Do you see any granite sets, small square blocks of granite, making a knobbly surface? These were used to stop the horses slipping.

Sometimes you will find smooth strips of stone or metal between the granite setts for wheels of carts to run over. Another thing to look for is a large stone block at the corner of a building. These are early crash barriers protecting the wall from carriage and cart wheels.

There are many other historic clues scattered around the streets and pavements of towns. Look at those below, and see how many you can find in your neighbourhood.

*Footscrapers for scraping mud off boots*

*Mosaic paving outside shops*

## Rubbing Coal-hole Covers

Find a cover in a reasonably quiet, dry place. Never make a rubbing in the road!

You will need: large sheets of paper, a soft brush, a wax crayon and some tape.

1 Brush off any loose grit.

2 Place a sheet of paper over the cover and tape down the edges.

3 Rub evenly over the paper with the **side** of the crayon until the pattern shows through.

4 Write on the paper where the cover was found, and what it was used for.

5 Store by rolling it up or placing it flat between boards.

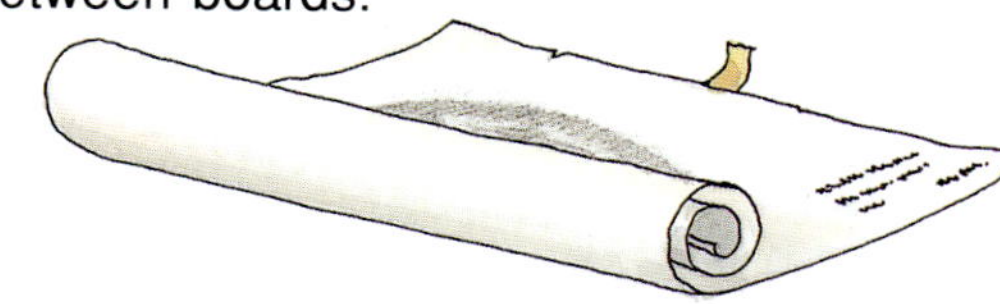

*Old paving revealed through the tarmac, a non-slip surface for horses and smooth setts for cart wheels*

*Coal-hole cover, and two sets of tiled steps*

# It's All in the Name

Have you ever wondered how your town got its name? Most English town names come from the language of the Anglo-Saxons. They were people who lived in England before the year 1100. Many of the word endings have a particular meaning.

| Word ending | Old English word | Meaning | Example |
|---|---|---|---|
| -bury | burg | fortified town | Salisbury |
| -ton | ton or tun | village or estate | Wolverhampton |
| -cester | ceaster | a fortified Roman town | Gloucester |
| -ham | ham | village | Birmingham |
| -wich | wic | workplace | Ipswich |
| -ley | leah | glade | Dudley |
| -ford | ford | ford(shallow river crossing) | Bradford |

The whole town name can be even more descriptive. Here are some examples:

OXFORD (Oxfordshire) Place at ford where oxen cross.

NEWHAVEN (East Sussex) Named after the new harbour built there in the sixteenth century.

SAFFRON WALDEN (Essex) The Anglo-Saxon word for Walden was Waladenu which meant 'the valley of the Britons'. Saffron grew there.

ABERYSTWYTH (Dyfed) Place at the mouth of the River Ystwyth.

NOTTINGHAM (Nottinghamshire) The village of Snotings, the people of Snota.

LIVERPOOL (Merseyside) Place at the pool with thick water.

BATH (Avon) Named after the Roman baths and hot springs.

HORSHAM (West Sussex) Enclosure where horses are kept. 'Hamm' meant enclosure.

HASLEMERE (Surrey) Place at the mere where hazels grow.

GOSPORT (Hampshire) The goose market. 'Port' meant market town.

GLASGOW (Strathclyde) The green hollow.

In your local library you will find books about the original meaning of place names. Find out as much as you can about your own town's name. Has it always been the same? Often spellings change over the years, but the meanings don't.

Street names can be just as interesting. They are often named after:

**geographical location** - East Street, North Road, Central Way;

**destination** - London Road, Glasgow Street, Gloucester Way;

**famous people** - King's Avenue, Victoria Street, Hamilton Terrace;

**natural environment** - Hill Road, Spring Hill, Beeches Way, Lake View;

**man-made environment** - Canal Street, Cathedral Close, Market Square, Church Walk, Dock Street;

**historical events** - Waterloo Street, Jubilee Way, Trafalgar Road.

Find examples from each of these categories in your own town. What do you think your own street is named after?

Buildings often have names too. Perhaps your home has a name. If not, what would you like to call it?

Blocks of flats have names. So do many factories, hospitals, shops, libraries, parks, pubs and office blocks.

Pub names can be particularly good fun to collect, especially on long car journeys.

Of course, people have names too. Do you know anyone whose surname is also a town name? You can find books about the origins of people's names. All names have origins, some more obvious than others. A good detective could find out most of them.

# Holy Revelations

Besides being places to worship God, churches are often full of clues to the past. The parish church is often the oldest building in the town.

Visit a local church (though not during a service). Sometimes churches are locked and you may have to ask for the key. A note in the porch should tell you where to get it.

Remember: Be quiet and calm inside churches. Do not run and shout around graveyards. Walk around graves, not over them.

At the church you should be able to find a leaflet about its history. Generations of people have added to or changed their churches. Can you find evidence of change? Different building styles? Perhaps some windows with rounded tops while others are pointed? Evidence of blocked-up arches. Walls built of different materials? Remains of old wall paintings? All these are clues to the history of the building.

*Even in the middle of busy town centres you may still find quiet churchyards like this one*

Look for decorations like gargoyles, carved pillars, and screens. There may even be an old sundial. A skilled historian can detect when these things were made by looking at and comparing the styles. It takes a lot of experience to do this, so start by just observing.

*Gargoyles are grotesquely -carved spouts carrying water away from gutters*

Churches generally have memorials to people who lived in the past. The obvious ones are gravestones. These give clues that you won't find elsewhere. They often show names of local families, who was related to whom, where they came from, and their occupations. Notice the different styles of tombstones and the lettering on them.

Look for a war memorial. These are often inside the church. Do you recognize any of the names? People often named their little boys after relations who were killed at war. It was another form of memorial. War memorials are the only memorials to all sorts of people, both rich and poor.

Wealthy people are often remembered by marble tombs and shiny brasses inside churches. Brasses are usually set into the floor, and may be covered by loose carpets to protect them from your feet.

## Making a Brass Rubbing

1 Find out whether the church has brasses.

2 You must ask permission from the vicar. You will find his name and address on a notice board.

3 Follow the instructions given on page 17 for making rubbings of coal-hole covers.

*A brass*

*A brass rubbing*

Instead of using a wax crayon, you could buy special crayons for brass rubbing from art and craft shops.

Try making rubbings in white, gold, or silver on to black paper.

If the edges of the rubbing are messy, or the paper is crumpled, cut carefully around the outline. Then stick the rubbing on to a clean piece of paper or board.

Old books and documents are often kept in churches. Parish registers have details of births, deaths, and marriages over many years. If you want to be a family history detective, these can be very valuable sources of information (your library will have books about how to trace family history). The vicar may also be able to show you old churchwardens' log books, church diaries, school records, or old letters.

# Time Lapse

Nothing stays the same for long. Things are changing all the time. You may be lucky enough to find a series of pictures of a particular place during different years. See how many changes you can spot in these photographs of crossroads.

After looking at the pictures below, try to find a similar set of pictures for your own town. Start by looking in your local museum or library. The librarian may be able to show you a box of old photographs. The local newspaper office would be a good place too; or search junk shops for old picture postcards.

# Your own Model Town

By making your own cardboard models you can create a street, neighbourhood, or whole town. Most buildings are fairly simple shapes, so it can be quite easy to make tiny models.

The easiest way to start is to use the templates. They must not be cut out of the book, but may be photocopied and coloured.

## Assembling your Models

**1** Make photocopies of the templates on thin card (or stick photocopies on card yourself). Make enlarged copies if you want to make bigger models.

**2** Colour in your copy, adding your own details.

**3** Cut out your model. The red outlines printed in the book show you which lines to cut on your own sheet.

**4** Now fold your model along the green lines shown in the book. It is best to score these first with the point of a pair of scissors.

**5** Put a little glue on all the flaps, as shown on the template by blue shading.

(TIP: cut a thin strip of waste card and use it to apply and spread the glue).

**6** Assemble the models as shown in the diagrams.

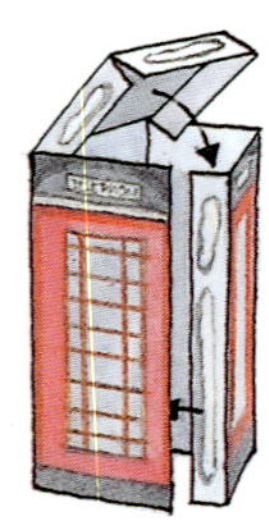

How about a telephone box against the wall of your church?

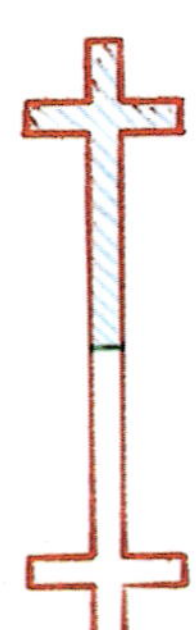

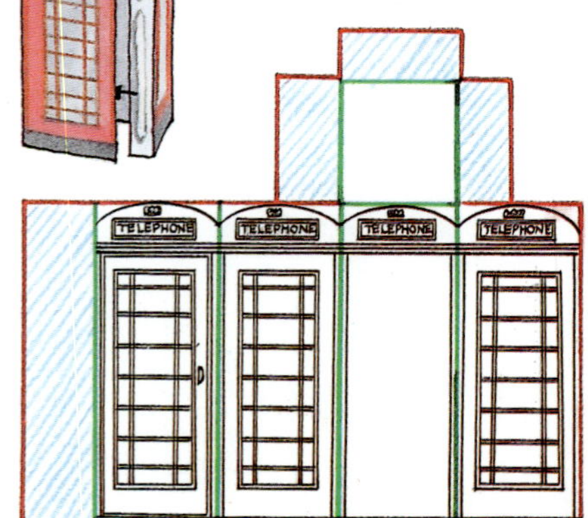

The finished model church

Try making buildings of different shapes

**A Church with a Spire**
Create your own tiny stained glass patterns.

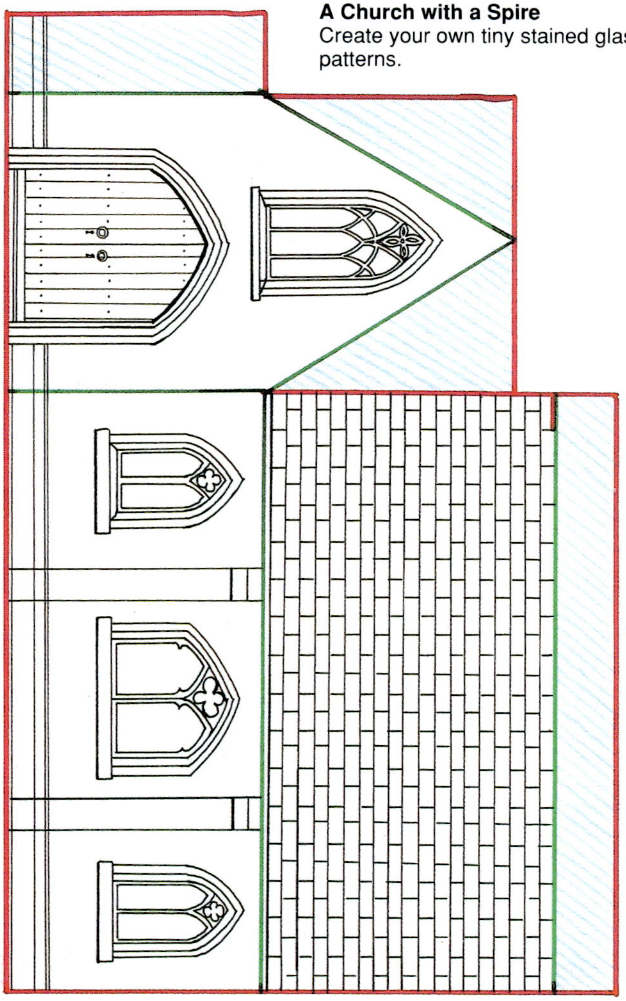

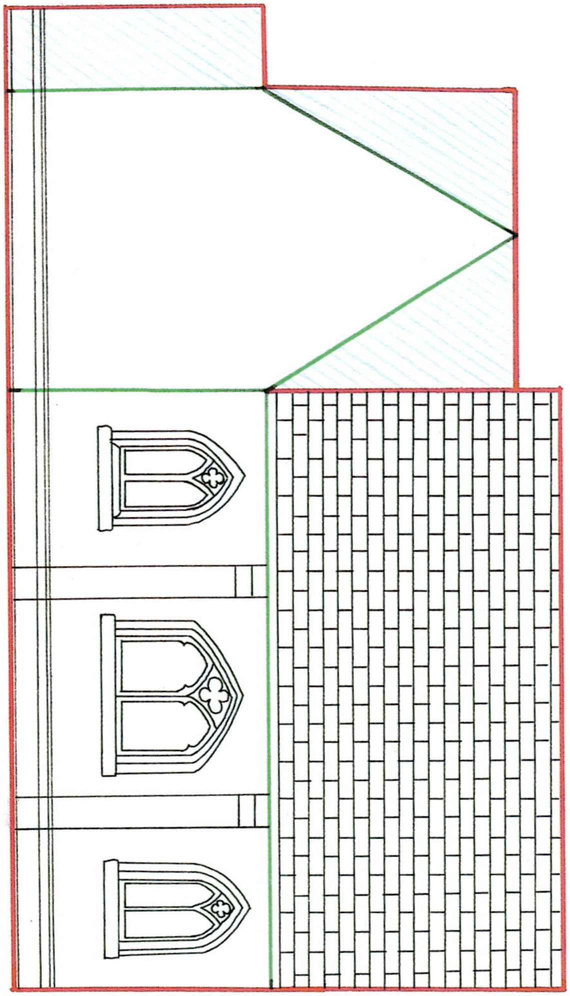

# Books to Read

*19th Century Buildings : Seekers' Notebooks* (Dinosaur Publications/ National Trust 1980)
*Church Memorial Brasses and Brass Rubbing,* Leigh Chapman (Shire Publications Ltd 1987)
*Homes,* John Platts (Macmillan 1972)
*Patterns of Living,* Michael Pollard (Holt, Rinehart & Winston 1985)
*On the Map,* David Boardman (BBC 1983)
*Moving into Maps,* J E Butler et al (Heineman Educational Books Ltd 1984)
*Discover Maps with Ordnance Survey,* Patricia & Steve Harrison (OS & Holmes McDougall 1988)
*Master Maps with Ordnance Survey,* Patricia & Steve Harrison (OS & Holmes McDougall 1988)
*Evidence Through Maps,* Bill Boyle (Collins Educational 1988)
*Maps & Map Games,* Deborah Manley (Piccolo/Pan 1976)
*On the Map,* David Boardman (BBC 1983)
*Local Directories,* Bill Boyle (Collins Educational 1987)
*In My Time,* John Cockcroft (Collins Educational 1986)
*Thanks for the Memory,* Sallie Purkis (Collins Educational 1987)
*Discovering Place Names,* John Field (Shire Publications Ltd 1976)
*The English Terrace House,* Stefan Multhesius (Yale University Press 1982)
*At Home in the 1930s,* Sallie Purkiss (Longman 1983)
*Basic Skills in Geography,* David Rose (Oxford 1988)
*How Old is Your House?* Pamela Cunnington (Alpha Books 1980)
*Discovering Your Old House,* David Iredale (Shire Publications Ltd 1977)
*History Around You,* L E Snellgrove (Oliver & Boyd 1983)
*Buildings,* David Woodlander (Collins Educational 1988)
*The Young Scientist Book of Archaeology,* Barbara Cork and Struan Reid (Usborne 1984)
*Suburban Style,* Helena Barrett & John Phillips (Macdonald Orbis 1987)
*How Towns Grow and Change,* Laurie Bolwell & Cliff Lines (Wayland 1985)

## Acknowledgements

**Photographs** Bob Seago: 5, 10 & 11, 21 (right), 25; Bill Launchbury 21 (left); The London Brass Rubbing Centre 21 (centre); Evening Argus 22 & 23 (left & centre). All other photographs: Lewis Cohen Urban Studies Centre at Brighton Polytechnic.
**Maps** Malcom Mason 12 & 13.
**Research Assistance** Denise Francis, Dicon Montford.

Selma Montford is the director of the Lewis Cohen Urban Studies Centre based at Brighton Polytechnic. It is an information and resource centre concerned with understanding the local environment.

There may be an Urban Studies Centre in your area; for a list of all Urban Studies Centres contact: the National Association for Urban Studies, Canterbury USC, 82 Alphege Lane, Canterbury, Kent CT1 2EB

# Index

A number in **bold** type means there is a picture